Mental TONIC

Richard Wilkins

10/10

With love

[signature]

First print 1998

Published by Cantecia
P O Box 454, Northampton NN4 0GJ

cantecia is an imprint of Ten out of Ten

ISBN 0 9528198 8 0

Cover design by Richard Wilkins
Printed by Candor Print, Northampton

DEDICATION

To John
my brother
my hero

In the whole of my life,
the most incredible sight I have ever seen,
was the awesome look of total wonderment,
love, joy and peace on your face
as heaven came to greet you.

You have made my life easy
now I know what awaits me.

INTRODUCTION

I'd decided to take my own life. I was recovering from a traumatic divorce, my company was at peak borrowing, then the recession struck. Almost over night I went from being a millionaire in a mansion to a bankrupt in a bedsit. I found myself alone, broke and terrified on Rock Bottom.

Today, I've never been richer. Not as in riches I own, but in riches I am. The difference is everything. These are riches that can never be taken, spent or lost, only shared, and the beauty is the more you give, the more you get.

So what happened to cause the massive change?... I simply overheard someone say, 'I'll get there'. These few words would change my whole life. THERE! I recalled how I was always going to get *there*. Although I'd been a self-made multi-millionaire living with my wife and children in a huge country mansion, driving not one but a fleet of Ferrari's, I'd never once felt I was *there*.

Of all places it was on Rock Bottom that I found *there*. I discovered *there* isn't where you think, it's **how** you think. I realised that you can't always change the things that affect you, but you can change the effect they have on you. I could see that there is no destination, the journey **is** the destination. I knew then the only thing that was hurting me was my resistance to change.

Words began to flow from my pen, it was like I was at the receiving end of some kind of cosmic fax. I began writing things I'd never known before. A book was born and so was I, into an exciting new way of thinking, which has since materialised many wonderful things into my life.

I owe much to Rock Bottom and those few simple words, 'I'll get *there*' You see it doesn't take a lot of words to make a big difference. Believe me, I know. This is the whole essence of this book, which used, could help you discover you're *there*.

Real change

is when you see the same old things
differently.

Treat yourself to a facelift -
Smile!

Status

is a gauge people use

to measure what isn't important.

Do you listen with the same enthusiasm
with which you speak?

Eternity starts before you die!

The part of you that notices
how old or how young,
how fat or how thin you are,
never changes.

You can't forget
what you won't forgive.

Grief

has opened many a heart
that happiness couldn't.

A comparison
is a sophisticated judgement.

It is impossible to create pressure
without resistance.

Possibility is the seed of the flower.

It must surely be an act of ignorance
to suppose that the same
organised intelligence
which created anything
as sophisticated as you and I,
could ever subject us
to something as barbaric as luck.

Achievement
is the amount of success
you allow yourself.

You must carry
what you won't let go.

Life's like a flower.
You have to push your way
through the top soil
and often some manure
before you get to blossom.

Confidence

is not being *without* fear -

It's not allowing it to control you.

Peace.

It doesn't happen to countries,

only people.

Friendship holds people together
when they are apart.

The reason many miss out
is because their priorities
are different to their dreams.

Personalities
are fittings,
not fixtures.

Try substituting the word **excitement**
for the word **fear.**

Whatever you blame
will control you.

Many a life
has been starved
by
the hunger for success.

How much do your opinions
allow for the feelings
of others?

Sacrifice

is the root of the flower.

Don't criticize God's work:

Love yourself!

The real art of listening,
is listening to those
who will not listen to you.

Depression

can be a wonderful gift,

concealed within a lousy wrapping.

The best place to have a party
is between your ears!

Selfishness
will always be rewarded
with discontentment.

The entire universe
in its awesome vastness,
important though it seems to us,
is just one of a billion cells
forming the wing of a butterfly
which settles on the petal of a flower
in one of many gardens
in a place called heaven.....

Enjoy the dreams of others
as well as those of your own.

Instant Karma:

Did you ever see an angry person
who was happy?

Passion

is the turbo boost on your life!

Use the past
as a library,
not a home.

Your self worth is measured
by your ability to receive
as much as your ability to give.

Many people will use up
a huge proportion of their lives
just trying to look different.

Happiness is a mood.

Contentment is a state of being.

Every action
marks the spot
where a thought once stood.

Global amnesia would stop all wars.

Patience

will always come to those who wait.

What do you hold onto the longest,
a criticism or a compliment?

Disappointment
is simply a dream
that doesn't want to become a reality.

You can't hold a hand
whilst you're holding a grudge.

People who think they won't achieve much,
rarely do.
People who think they *will* achieve much,
rarely don't.

Compromise

is the shape of water.

Pain
has created more love songs
than happiness.

The one who whispers
will draw people closer
than the one who shouts.

Only your lack of trust
will ever stop you letting go.

You have made important
whatever offends you.

A co-incidence
is an earthly reply
to a cosmic fax
you sent earlier!

Don't be obsessed
to live as *long* as you can -
but as *well* as you can.

Age is not as noticeable
on a face of character.

Anger is a breeding ground for illness.

People who reach out
will always touch more.

If you need directions,
don't ask someone who's lost...

The willow does not owe its beauty to the oak,

nor the oak its acorns to the willow.

Yet together, in their separateness,

they create a huge oneness.

The forest.

Much of the beauty of life is missed
by people who are busy
seeking the approval of others.

If your living room window is grubby,
you don't go out and polish the view!

Wonderment
is when you see something
without looking through a belief.

Harmful
Attitude
To
Experience

Pain gives birth to miracles!
Ask any mother.

Increase your odds...

Don't wait for what's around the corner.

Go and look around as many as you can!

You don't find treasure on the surface.

Laughter

is the dance of the spirit.

Why should anyone like you,

if you don't?

Miracles start to happen
when you give as much energy
to your dreams
as you do to your fears.

You can grow big and strong
without eating meat.
Ask any tree!

See an act of God.

Look in a mirror!

You can change what you see,
if you change how you look.

A big personality
carries far more weight
than a thin body.

Do you listen
or wait to talk?

The imagination
is a dream factory
of which realities
are a by-product.

Fun

is often traded for ambition.

Self esteem
is an unnecessary ingredient
in an abusive relationship.

Allow your words
to pass first through your ears
before allowing them out of your mouth.

A lesson can never be taught,
only learned.

It's the space between the walls
which gives the room its size.

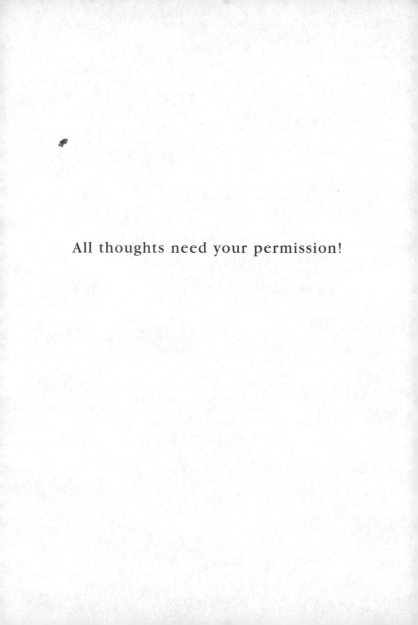

All thoughts need your permission!

A tiny light
can break through a huge darkness,
yet a huge darkness
cannot break through a tiny light.

What if we've got it wrong,
and everything is right?

You don't doubt there's a road,
just because it disappears around the bend
and out of sight.

When I was young
I thought I could change the world...
now I'm old,
I know I can.

Life:
Many people are too busy
struggling with the stairs,
to notice there's a lift.

Gossip

is an oral infection!

Forgiveness frees the forgiver,
far more than the forgiven.

Regret

is a lesson

you are still learning.

Inexperience
often triumphs over experience
because it doesn't know where to fail.

Don't devalue your life
by not appreciating it!

Parents

are responsible for your birth

....not your life.

Why allow harsh words to use your tongue?

Hypocrisy is invisible only to its user.

The measure of your greatest moment
is its distance from your worst.

Until you change,
the same old problems
will keep turning up
wearing different clothes.

Anger
is your intolerance
made public!

Don't use up your life
as a profit making exercise.

Your body is the car
which takes you through life.
One day the car will be scrapped...
but that isn't the end of the driver,
...is it!

It's no co-incidence
that the ideal praying position
is when you're on your knees.

What matters is how it affects you,
not how it is.

Prosperity

is a by-product of

persistence.

There are two ways to heaven...
One is when you really die.
The other when you really live.

A healthy body
is of little use
to an unhealthy mind.

When you are unattached to the outcome,
there is no risk.

Work can only start
where you allow your enjoyment to finish.

Enthusiasm
negates
effort!

Dying people
never use calculators
to evaluate their lives.

Time stops
when you are doing what you love.

You can't fight a statistic,
but you *can* beat it.

How much you get from life
will depend on your self worth,
not your circumstances.

Real wealth

is when you *give* your time to people,

not *sell* it for money.

Wonderful things happen...

when you dare to dream outside of sleep.

Alcohol will tell you she's a beautiful mist.

Wisdom knows she's a dangerous fog.

Kindness is like hate:
You can't give it
without a little rubbing off on yourself.

God causes rain to fall on the flower,
not because he wants it to be
wet and miserable,
but because he wants it to grow.

Negative situations
are accelerators of appreciation.

Why wait to get out of life
what you've put in?...

Just enjoy putting in!

Stubbornness
has caused many a soul
to miss the song.

With every breath
comes the opportunity
to see something differently.

Through your prayers
you can influence **anything**.

Paradise

is a consciousness

not a continent.

We would appreciate our lives more
if the starving
got as much publicity
as the rich.

If you awoke holding a rose
which you had picked in a dream,
you would marvel at it.
You would show it to all your friends.
You would keep it.
You would treasure that rose.
The world is full of roses...

Ignorance

is a very thin shell

concealing much wisdom.

Time changes a face back to how it was
before infatuation placed its mask over it.

Moods...
are the many different coloured filters
through which we can view
the same situation.

Maturity
is growing wiser
not older.

Never realise a dream
until you have another
to put in its place.

If you want an incentive
to change your life.
Visit the future now,
to see how it will be
if you don't!

Cynicism

is the fear of trust.

Importance:

It never comes *with* situations,

we attach it.

There is little understanding
to be learned
from a trouble free existence.

It's hard to remove the stain
a single lie can leave.

Many a family has been neglected
by the excuse
of providing for the family.

You may *want* to change.

But are you ready?

Making a living
is rarely as rewarding
as making a difference.

The most powerful way to love
is to love yourself,
then encourage others to do the same.

A breakdown
is often the beginning
of a breakthrough.

Only what you refuse to accept
will ever be a problem.

The more we own
reflects
<u>not</u>
protects
our insecurity.

Expanding on what is right
instantly gives less space
to what isn't.

Prejudices
are the strings
which control the puppet.

God made the world round
so it wouldn't have any sides.

It's the silence
between the notes
that creates the music.

Why take the trouble to be kind...
when you can take the pleasure?

Frustration
doesn't happen
when you *don't* want things
your way!

Stars are Gods reminders
that we see the furthest
when it's dark.

Hanging on
requires far more effort
than
letting go.

Faith

is a river

on which many a dream has sailed home.

Most people die without really living.

(Don't be one of them!)

Assuming the popular belief,
that there really is a heaven
and we really do have all of eternity,
one thing is for certain
and not open to doubt.
The best is yet to come!

ACKNOWLEDGMENTS

To the many thousands of people
who have purchased my books.

To the organisers of the talks
at which I've been privileged to speak.

To the people who have given their time
to hear me speak.

To those in the media who have helped me
reach millions of people.

To the many who have written letters
which have humbled me.

To the people who have encouraged me,
many without even knowing it.

Every one of you has given me a piece of yourself,
...everything is energy, I can feel it, I will use it.

'To appreciate' means: *to increase in value*

Many people wish they had appreciated more. For this reason, I wrote....

'I want to love you now.'

I want to love you now,
I want to appreciate and never take our love for granted.

I want to love you now,
not from regret of what once was and is no more.

I want to love you now,
And thank God for your birth
and see all else you do as a bonus to my life.

I want to love you now,
not after making up from some fall out,
but in the middle of that fall out.

I want to love you now,
whilst I am able to feel your fingers curl around my hand.

I want to love you now,
and let both our tears of joy and sorrow
flow as a single river of understanding.

I want to love you now,
enough to notice a single strand of your hair
that waves out to me on a windy day.

I want to love you now,
not through painful memories trying to escape a broken heart.

I want to love you now,
even when you are too busy to notice me loving you.

I want to love you now,
not through tear stained photos of good times we once had.

I want to love you now,
not through the grief of death, but in the time we have today.

Not some day too late,
I want to love you now.

Richard is regularly invited to speak
at venues around the country.
His talks are profound, passionate and very funny.
For details of Richards upbeat talks
and forthcoming publications,
please write to the address below.

10/10

The Inner Nutshell Cards

... 60 small inspirational cards each with a quotation
taken from Richard's first three books.

150 ways to make your life
Ten out of Ten

... Richard's first book of quotations.

10 out of 10
The Yellow Book

... Richard's second book of quotations.

*If you are unable to obtain any of the above,
they can be purchased from:*

Ten out of Ten
PO Box 454
Northampton NN4 0GJ

£4,99 each plus 50p per item p&p.